KIJC
1/12

LANGUAGE-ARTS EXPLORER

THE BIRTH OF THE UNITED STATES

1754 to the 1820s

IN CONGRESS, JULY 4, 1776.

The unanimous Declaration of the thirteen united States of America,

by Linda Crotta Brennan

HISTORY DIGS

CHERRY LAKE PUBLISHING • ANN ARBOR, MICHIGAN

CHERRY LAKE
Publishing

Published in the United States of America
by Cherry Lake Publishing
Ann Arbor, Michigan
www.cherrylakepublishing.com

Printed in the United States of America
Corporate Graphics Inc
September 2011
CLFA09

Consultants: Brett Barker, associate professor of history, University of Wisconsin–Marathon County; Gail Saunders-Smith, associate professor of literacy, Beeghly College of Education, Youngstown State University

Editorial direction:
Melissa York

Design and production:
Marie Tupy

Photo credits: National Archives and Records Administration, cover, 1, 14; Paul Revere/Library of Congress, 5, 8; North Wind Picture Archives, 7, 17, 19; American Memory/Library of Congress, 10; Currier & Ives/Library of Congress, 11; Hulton Archive/Getty Images, 13; Anne S. K. Brown Military Collection/Brown University Library, 21; Library of Congress, 23; National Archives and Records Administration, 24; Jeffrey M. Frank/Shutterstock Images, 27; Fotolia, 30

Library of Congress Cataloging-in-Publication Data
Brennan, Linda Crotta.
The birth of the United States / by Linda Crotta Brennan.
   p. cm. – (Language arts explorer–History digs)
ISBN 978-1-61080-197-3 – ISBN 978-1-61080-285-7 (pbk.)
1. United States–History–Revolution, 1775-1783–Juvenile literature. I. Title.
E208.B84 2011
973.3–dc22

                       2011015122

Cherry Lake Publishing would like to acknowledge the work of The Partnership for 21st Century Skills. Please visit www.21stCenturySkills.org for more information.

TABLE OF CONTENTS

You are being given a mission. The facts in What You Know will help you accomplish it. Remember the clues from What You Know while you are reading the story. The clues and the story will help you answer the questions at the end of the book. Have fun on this adventure!

YOUR MISSION

Your mission is to learn to think like a historian. What tools do historians use to research the past? What kinds of questions do they ask, and where do they look for answers? On this assignment, your goal is to learn about the Revolutionary War. What were the causes of the war? How did the war affect the people of that time? How did the war influence the kind of government the United States has now? Keep the What You Know facts in mind as you read.

WHAT YOU KNOW

★ Before the Revolutionary War, America was a **colony** of Britain. King George III of England was the ruler.

★ Not all Americans were Patriots who wanted independence. Some remained Loyalists. They didn't want to be separate from Britain.

★ Before the Revolutionary War, America was a loose collection of 13 colonies. Each colony had its own government.

★ After the Revolutionary War, the United States of America became an independent country.

★ As an independent country, the United States needed to change from 13 colonies to 13 states with one government.

Paul Revere printed this image of the Boston Massacre, which happened on March 5, 1770. British soldiers fired into a Boston mob, causing what are considered the first deaths in the American Revolution.

A student reporter is visiting the local history museum. The museum **curator** is setting up an exhibit about the Revolutionary War. Learn to explore history as a historian might by reading the reporter's interview with the curator.

Today I'm at the museum with the curator, Mr. Rosa. We enter a room filled with boxes. I help Mr. Rosa slide a large picture frame out of a box. An old map is mounted inside.

"What's this?" I ask him. "It looks like America, but it doesn't have all of the states."

"It's a map of the original 13 British colonies at the time of the Revolutionary War," explains Mr. Rosa.

We hang the map on the wall and straighten the frame.

"What's the Northwest Territory?" I ask, pointing to an area west of the colonies.

"It became a U.S. territory in 1784, but the British won the region from the French in an earlier war," says Mr. Rosa. "From 1754 to 1763, Britain fought a war with France. The British called it the Seven Years' War. Americans called it the French and Indian War. When Britain won, France gave Britain the Ohio River Valley and Canada."

THE 13 COLONIES

The 13 original colonies were New Hampshire, Massachusetts, Rhode Island, Connecticut, New York, New Jersey, Pennsylvania, Delaware, Maryland, Virginia, North Carolina, South Carolina, and Georgia. Today's state of Maine was part of the Massachusetts colony. Vermont was part of the New York colony, and West Virginia was part of the Virginia Colony.

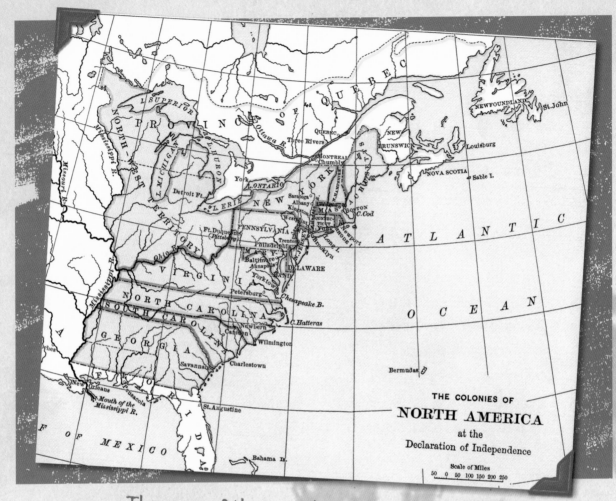

The names of the original 13 colonies are familiar, but many had different boundaries than the modern states do today.

I frown. That's not the war I came to learn about. "What does all of this have to do with the Revolutionary War?"

"It all came down to taxes," says Mr. Rosa. "Let me explain."

Money and Soldiers

"Even though Britain won, the French and Indian War cost a lot of money. Britain needed to raise taxes to pay their debt. And they also needed money to pay more soldiers."

"Why did they need soldiers if the war was over?" I ask.

"The British were afraid that the Indians and the French in America would cause more trouble. So the British sent nearly 10,000 soldiers back to America."

Taxation without Representation

"The British **Parliament** passed laws taxing Americans to pay for these soldiers," Mr. Rosa explains.

"Before this, Americans had only been taxed by their local colonial governments. Now they were being taxed by a Parliament in England 3,000 miles away. Americans had no representative in Parliament. They had no say in how they were taxed. They didn't think this was fair.

"To fight the taxes, Americans **boycotted** British goods. British merchants lost money. They complained to Parliament and got the tax laws **repealed**."

I look over my notes. "Wasn't everything okay once Britain repealed the tax laws?"

"Not exactly," Mr. Rosa tells me. "Parliament passed new taxes. British troops were stationed in Boston to enforce the laws and on March 5, 1770, a large mob of Bostonians faced off against a small group of British soldiers. The soldiers fired into the crowd, killing five people. We call this event the Boston Massacre, and it was only the beginning of the unrest in the city. I'll explain more tomorrow when we unpack the Boston Tea Party box." ★

I return the next day to help Mr. Rosa. He's lifting a heavy box onto his worktable when I enter the room.

"Will this tea party include a cake?" I ask him.

"I'm afraid not," he says. "This was a different kind of party. It was more what we'd call a protest."

I remember yesterday's discussion. "Did it have to do with taxes?"

"Indeed it did." Mr. Rosa nods. "Parliament passed a Tea Act. It allowed the British East India Company to sell cheap tea to Americans. But there was a tax on the tea. Americans saw this as a trick to make them accept Parliament's tax."

We pry open the box.

Mr. Rosa carefully lifts out a yellowed sheet of paper and places it in a glass case. "This broadside was posted all over Boston, Massachusetts, after the Tea Act was passed."

I lean closer to read the broadside. In part, it says, "THIS is to Remind the Publick, That it was solemnly voted by the Body of the

BROADSIDES

Broadsides were signs printed on one side of a piece of paper. In the days of the Revolutionary War, there was no Internet, telephone, radio, or television. The American colonies had few newspapers, and the news in them was often months old. To pass along information, people posted broadsides in village gathering places.

Boston patriots printed this notice shortly
before the Boston Tea Party.

People of this and the neighbouring Towns . . . that the said Tea never should be landed in this Province . . . "

I notice the date of the broadside, December 2, 1773. "It sounds like they were very angry," I comment. "What did they want?"

"They were indeed," agrees Mr. Rosa. "The broadside is warning the people of Boston not to buy tea. This was printed right before things got ugly. On December 16, 1773, the people of Boston met together. They sent a message to the royal governor, who had been appointed by King George. The people told the royal governor that they wouldn't pay the tax on tea. They demanded that the ships take the tea back to Britain. The royal governor refused to give in to their demands. Then someone shouted, 'Boston Harbor a Teapot Tonight!'"

I jot that down. "What did it mean?"

"It was a secret signal," Mr. Rosa tells me, "arranged by a group of men called the Sons of Liberty. They thought of themselves as Patriots protecting America's freedom."

A Sea of Tea

"That night a group of Patriots blackened their faces. They disguised themselves as American Indians. They boarded the ships and brought the heavy tea chests onto the decks," Mr. Rosa explains.

Mr. Rosa shows me a large dark wooden box. "This is a **replica** of one of those tea chests. See where a Patriot chopped it open with a hatchet? The Patriots dumped all of the tea into the sea."

"Didn't that get the Patriots in trouble?" I ask.

"Since they were in disguise, no one knew who they were," Mr. Rosa says, "but King George and the Parliament were furious. Parliament passed a law to punish Boston. It closed down the harbor until the people of Boston had paid for the lost tea.

"Then King George sent more British soldiers to Boston to enforce the law. Any Americans caught smuggling food or other goods into Boston would be arrested. They would be sent to Britain to be tried without a jury."

I frown. "But then the people of Boston might starve."

"King George was sure that would force Boston to accept the tax and pay for the tea," Mr. Rosa explains. ★

Entry 3: THE DECLARATION OF INDEPENDENCE

I'm back today to learn about the First Continental Congress and the Declaration of Independence. I ask Mr. Rosa if King George's idea of shutting down Boston Harbor worked.

Continental Congress

"No, it didn't," Mr. Rosa says. "Instead, the other colonies worked together to help Boston. They sent **delegates** to a meeting called the Continental Congress beginning in 1774.

"Soon the Continental Congress became the colonists' government." Mr. Rosa shows me a model of a brick building with a high bell tower. "The delegates met here, at Carpenter's Hall in Philadelphia, Pennsylvania.

"At first, the Continental Congress wrote to King George to explain their problems. They hoped they could come to an agreement with the king. But he refused to **compromise**," explains Mr. Rosa.

"The Continental Congress decided talking couldn't solve the problem with Britain. In April 1775, open warfare broke out between

VISITING HISTORY

Many of the buildings from the time of the Revolutionary War are still standing. In Philadelphia, you can visit the State House, also known as Independence Hall, where the Declaration of Independence was signed. In Boston, you can see the Old South Meeting House, where the Tea Party meeting took place, and Bunker Hill, the site of one of the first battles of the war.

the Patriots and the British. The first battles were at Lexington and Concord, Massachusetts. By the summer of 1776, the Continental Congress had decided that the King would never listen to their demands and respect their rights, so independence was their only option. Thomas Jefferson was chosen to write the Declaration of Independence," Mr. Rosa tells me.

The Declaration

I tap my pencil. "What did it say?"

"I have a replica of an early copy here." Mr. Rosa takes a yellowed document out of the box. He sets it up on its own stand. "When Thomas Jefferson wrote the Declaration of Independence, he tried to

This is a copy of a famous painting by John Trumbull showing the signing of the Declaration of Independence. The original hangs in the U.S. Capitol.

explain the colonists' reasons for breaking away. He wrote about the ideals that were important to Americans," Mr. Rosa explains.

I lean closer and read out loud.

"We hold these truths to be self-evident, that all men are created equal, that they are endowed by their Creator with certain unalienable rights, that among these are life, liberty and the pursuit of happiness."

Then it told King George about the colonists' complaints. It ends,

"We, therefore, the representatives of the United States of America . . . do, in the name, and by the authority of the good people of these colonies . . . declare, that these united colonies are, and of right ought to be free and independent states."

"What did this end part mean?" I ask.

"Basically it meant that the colonies didn't belong to Britain any more," Mr. Rosa says. "They were their own separate country.

"Delegates from all 13 colonies signed the Declaration of Independence. Then they rang the bell." Mr. Rosa points to the cracked bell in the tower of the Pennsylvania State House. "We call that the Liberty Bell now. Patriots all over Philadelphia cheered the birth of their new country—the United States of America."

"Was it that easy?" I ask. "The United States was born just like that?"

"Not exactly," answers Mr. Rosa. "Britain was not going to let its colonies go so easily. The colonists would have to fight for their independence." ★

Today Mr. Rosa is setting up an exhibit about what life was like for Americans during the Revolutionary War. The war continued for years and affected the lives of everyone in the colonies. He shows me an old leather-bound book.

Loyalists and Patriots

"This is Mary Gould Almy's diary," says Mr. Rosa. "It's on loan from another museum. Careful, it's very delicate."

"Mary?" I ask. "She wasn't a soldier, was she?"

"No," says Mr. Rosa, "but she went through a battle. Mary and her six children lived in Newport, Rhode Island. Her town was occupied by the British. Mary's husband was away, fighting for the Patriots. But Mary didn't agree with her husband. She was a Loyalist."

I underline that word in my notes. "What was a Loyalist?"

WOMEN'S RIGHTS

It was unusual for a woman like Mary Almy to disagree with her husband. At the time, women did not have political rights of their own—they could not vote, and their fathers and then their husbands controlled their property and made many of their decisions. Women fought for more rights throughout the nineteenth century and into the twentieth century. Women finally gained the right to vote in the United States in 1920.

"A Loyalist was a colonist who was still loyal to King George," Mr. Rosa explains. "Mary didn't think the colonists had the right to break away from Britain. Many colonists were Loyalists.

"Mary had friends and relatives on both sides of the war. That was very hard for her. She wrote in her diary about living through a battle between the Patriots and the British. Read her description of the fight," Mr. Rosa says, pointing to the page.

> All was horror and confusion . . . How many [unhappy] families were made that day. . . . Some of my good friends in the front of the battle here; and Heaven only knows how many of the other side. . . . I trembled for fear they would say, your husband lies among the slain, or that he is wounded and a prisoner.

Living through War

"What happened to Mary and her husband?" I ask.

"They both survived the war," Mr. Rosa tells me. "But while it was going on, Mary and her children had hard times. They barely had enough food to eat. They didn't have enough wood to keep warm. By the end of the war, all the trees in Newport had been chopped down, and people had started to take apart houses for fuel." ★

Today Mr. Rosa is setting up an exhibit about the life of a Revolutionary War soldier. I help him dress a mannequin in breeches and a white shirt with fringes around the collar and edges.

Food and Clothes

"This is called a hunting shirt," he explains. "Most Patriot soldiers wore one. Many of them were linen, like this one. After months of fighting, these shirts got pretty worn."

I remember that the British wore red coats. "What color coats did the Patriots wear?"

A later artist imagined this soldier standing duty during the winter of 1777–1778 at Valley Forge, Pennsylvania.

"Most Patriot soldiers didn't get coats," Mr. Rosa tells me.

I figure the Patriots must have been awfully cold in winter. We wrap the mannequin's feet in rags.

"Didn't the soldiers have shoes?" I ask as I make a quick sketch.

Mr. Rosa tucks in the end of a rag and stands up. "Yes, most of them wore moccasins or another type of leather shoe, but soldiers did so much walking, their shoes wore out. Then the soldiers had to walk barefoot, even in the snow."

The thought makes me shiver. "Did the Patriots have enough to eat?"

"They were supposed to get regular rations of meat, flour, and other food. But supplies didn't always reach them. Often they went hungry."

Sickness

I stare at our shabby looking Patriot. "If the Patriots were so hungry and cold, did many get sick?"

Mr. Rosa nods. "With so many soldiers living so close together, germs spread rapidly. Illness was a big problem. We estimate that for

VACCINES

Patriot doctors knew one method that often stopped the spread of one deadly disease—smallpox. They had learned that if they gave healthy men a shot with a weak form of smallpox, the men would usually develop a resistance against the disease. Today, vaccines protect people against many diseases such as polio, measles, and the flu.

every soldier killed in battle, ten more died from disease."

"Didn't they have doctors to take care of the soldiers?" I ask.

"They did, but sometimes the doctors did more harm than good. They didn't know about germs or what caused diseases back then."

Mr. Rosa takes out a wooden box with a handle. "This was a medicine chest. It is similar to the chests carried by doctors with the Patriot troops."

Mr. Rosa shows me the compartments inside and opens one of the drawers. He takes out some of the instruments and explains how they were used. "These **forceps** were for removing bullets. This curved needle was used for sewing up wounds. This is a lancet. It was a special knife used to make a patient bleed."

Yuck, I think. "Why would a doctor make a patient bleed?" I ask.

"In those days doctors thought that illness was caused by an imbalance in the body," explains Mr. Rosa. "To put the body back in balance, doctors sometimes bled their patients. Or they might give them medicines to make them vomit. Or smear their patients with a paste that gave them blisters."

"Didn't that stuff make the patient sicker?" I ask.

"Often it did," Mr. Rosa tells me.

I flip through my notes. "If a soldier's life was so hard, who would sign up to be one?"

"People who felt freedom was more important than comfort or safety," Mr. Rosa says. "Patriots came in all different ages, sizes, and colors. Tomorrow we'll talk more about that." ★

Today I'm helping Mr. Rosa set up an exhibit about black soldiers in the Revolutionary War.

Black Patriots

Mr. Rosa places a long list of names in a glass case. "This is a muster roll—a list of the Patriots who fought at the battles of Lexington and Concord." He points to a number of the names. "Peter Salem, Pomp Blackman, Job Potamia—these were all black soldiers."

I peer at the names. "Black, so that means these men were African Americans?"

"Many of them were, but some of the men who were called black were actually American Indian," he says. "And some were of mixed race. For example, Crispus Attucks, who was killed by British soldiers in the Boston Massacre, was Natick Indian, African, and European."

I look up from writing. "Did a lot of black men fight for the Patriots during the Revolutionary War?"

"Quite a few," Mr. Rosa tells me. "Approximately 5,000 black Patriot soldiers fought."

Differences between the North and South

"Did most of the black Patriots come from the South?" I ask.

"No, actually, most came from the North," Mr. Rosa says. "Before the Revolutionary War, there was slavery in the North, too. Not all black Patriots were slaves, though. Some were free men."

"Did any black men from the South fight?"

This is one of the earliest known images
of a black Revolutionary War soldier.

"Many Southern slave owners were against allowing slaves to fight," Mr. Rosa explains. "They were afraid armed slaves might turn on their owners. But sometimes an owner sent his slave to fight in his place. Slaves fought for the British, too, because the British promised them freedom."

After the War

"What happened to the black Patriots after the war?" I ask.

"In the South, most of them remained slaves. Some who were especially heroic were awarded their freedom. Most Northern black soldiers were given their freedom. The Revolutionary War changed the way people felt about slavery in the North."

"What do you mean?" I ask.

End to Northern Slavery

"Men who fought for freedom felt uneasy with slavery," Mr. Rosa explains. "Dr. Harris was a white Patriot who had fought beside black soldiers during the Revolutionary War. He gave a speech about slavery. Here's a recording of an actor reading Dr. Harris' speech." Mr. Rosa points to a CD player on a shelf and asks me to push the play button.

> Then liberty, independence, freedom, were in every man's mouth. They were the sounds at which they rallied, and under which they fought and bled . . . The word slavery then filled their hearts with horror. They fought because they would not be slaves.

Mr. Rosa explains, "After the Revolutionary War, the Northern states got rid of slavery in the North. But slavery would continue in the South until after the Civil War, which ended in 1865." ★

SEGREGATION IN THE ARMY

After the Revolutionary War, the Unites States Armed Services were segregated. That meant African American and white troops were kept in separate units. The army did not begin to integrate African Americans with white troops again until 1948. Today, the U.S. Armed Services are integrated.

Today we are setting up the final portion of the exhibit. It's about the Constitution of the United States.

Country Divided

I flip open my notebook. "So America won the Revolutionary War and then we were a country, right?"

Mr. Rosa shakes his head and smiles. "It wasn't that easy. At first the 13 states were only loosely joined. Each state acted almost like its own country. That didn't work very well."

Mr. Rosa shows me an old handwritten letter. "This is a letter that George Washington wrote to his friend John Jay. Washington was very discouraged. The United States was dissolving into 13 squabbling states. Washington was worried that everything he and his men had fought for in the Revolutionary War would be destroyed."

I read the letter.

> *Dear Sir,*
> *The [country] we have been seven years raising at the expense of much blood and treasure must fall . . . Thirteen [states] pulling against each other . . . will soon bring ruin on the whole. We are either a United people or we are not . . . let us act as a nation.*

Mr. Rosa puts the letter carefully in a glass case. "In order to be united, we needed to figure out a new form of government. So, in 1787, delegates from all but one of the states met for a Constitutional Convention."

I'm surprised. "Which state didn't go?"

"Rhode Island. They were worried about losing their independence," Mr. Rosa tells me. "Americans had fought to overthrow Britain and King George. Many were afraid that if they established a strong central government, they would just be exchanging one king for another."

"Was it hard to get everyone to agree on a new government?"

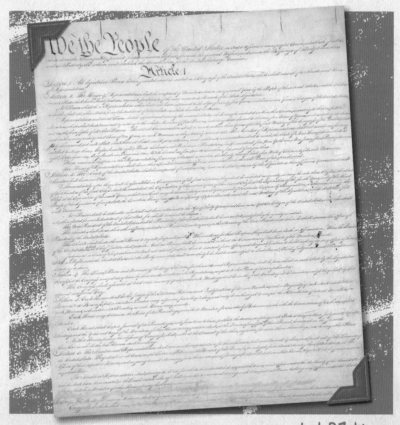

The U.S. Constitution has been amended 27 times.

"Indeed it was," Mr. Rosa says. "Some Americans wanted power to stay with the states. Others felt the power needed to be in the central government."

"Which side won?" I ask.

"Both," says Mr. Rosa. "They came up with a compromise. The Constitution balances power between the states and the central government. Power is also divided between the executive, legislative, and judicial branches of government."

"That sounds like a pretty good arrangement," I say.

"But some people still weren't satisfied," Mr. Rosa tells me. "They wanted to make sure the rights of the people were protected. So we added ten amendments to the Constitution, called the Bill of Rights. Some of the rights guaranteed our freedom of religion, freedom of speech, and the right to a fair trial."

"Do we still have the same form of government today?" I ask.

"Yes we do." Mr. Rosa holds up a copy of the Constitution and the Bill of Rights. "This is what made all the hardship of the Revolutionary War worthwhile." ★

THE U.S. GOVERNMENT TODAY

The United States still has the same three branches of government today. The executive branch is headed by the president. He or she is the leader of the country and commands the military. The legislative branch consists of the Senate and the House of Representatives. They write the laws. The judicial branch is made up of the country's courts. They decide how the laws will be applied.

MISSION ACCOMPLISHED!

Congratulations! You have read documents and examined objects from the past. You have asked the same kinds of questions historians ask. As you did so, you learned about the Revolutionary War. You discovered Americans fought because they felt their rights were abused by the British Parliament and King George III. You learned that not all Americans wanted to break away from Britain. You discovered that life was hard for families and soldiers during the war. You found out that American Indian and African American soldiers fought in the Revolutionary War. You learned that the founders of the United States made sure our Constitution balanced power and protected the rights of the people. Great job!

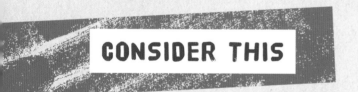

CONSIDER THIS

★ Why did some colonists stay loyal to the British king?

★ What do you think freedom and liberty meant to the colonists? How did people of different genders and races experience freedom and liberty in the colonies? What do these words mean to you?

★ Why do people protest the actions of their governments? What issue do you feel strongly enough about to attend a protest?

You can visit Independence Hall in Philadelphia,
where the Declaration of Independence was signed.
What does independence mean to you?

GLOSSARY

boycott (BOI-kaht) to protest something by refusing to use, buy, or deal with it

colony (KAH-luh-nee) a territory belonging to and ruled by a distant nation

compromise (KAHM-pruh-mize) to make an agreement that has only some of what each side wanted

curator (KYOOR-ay-tur) the person who chooses and organizes the items in museum displays

delegate (DEL-i-git) a person chosen to speak or act as a representative for others

forceps (FOR-seps) a tool used to hold or grip things, especially in delicate operations

Parliament (PAHR-luh-muhnt) a group of people who make a country's laws

repeal (ri-PEEL) to get rid of officially

replica (REP-li-kuh) an exact copy of something

BOOKS

Brennan, Linda. *The Black Regiment of the American Revolution.*
Bedford, NH: Apprentice Shop Books, 2008.

Haugen, David, ed. *Voices of the Revolutionary War: Soldiers.*
San Diego, CA: Blackbirch Press, 2004.

Ratliff, Thomas M. *How to Be a Revolutionary War Soldier.*
Washington DC: National Geographic, 2008.

WEB SITES

Ben's Guide to US Government for Kids History of the Constitution
http://bensguide.gpo.gov/6-8/documents/constitution/background.html

This Web site explains how lawmakers compromised to write the
U.S. Constitution.

Black Soldiers and Sailors During the Revolution
http://www.earlyamerica.com/review/2004_summer_fall/soldiers.htm

This Web site provides more information about the experiences of
black soldiers during the Revolutionary War.

FURTHER MISSIONS

MISSION 1

The men who created the Constitution felt that state power was important. Find out more about your state government. Do you have a representative in state government? Who is it? Who is your governor?

MISSION 2

The Bill of Rights protects your right to petition your government.

Is there an issue that is important to you? Can you write to your local or national government about it? Perhaps you can find a way to improve things in your town or city.

The original Liberty Bell is still on display in Philadelphia, though the crack down its front prevents it from being rung.

INDEX

ABOUT THE AUTHOR

Linda Crotta Brennan taught elementary school and worked in a library. She has her master's degree in Early Childhood Education. Now she is a full-time writer. She writes about history and nature. She lives with her husband and golden retriever in Rhode Island. She has three grown daughters.

ABOUT THE CONSULTANTS

Brett Barker is an associate professor of history at the University of Wisconsin–Marathon County in Wausau. He received his PhD in history from the University of Wisconsin–Madison and his MA and BA in history from Ohio State University. He has also worked with K–12 teachers in two Teaching American History grants.

Gail Saunders-Smith is a former classroom teacher and Reading Recovery teacher leader. Currently, she teaches literacy courses at Youngstown State University in Ohio. Gail is the author of many books for children and three professional books for teachers.